What Others Are Saying about This Book . . .

Terrell Carter offers a thought address-
ing racism and police-citizen i   ons. His
unique insight as a former police   iinister,
as well as a community activist, ...ng on all
sides of these issue which can bri__... ... divides—and point the way to
a more hopeful future. —**Zach Dawes, Managing Editor,** *Ethics Daily*

We have much to do about how police patrol minorities communities and how the criminal justice system reviews officer-involved fatal
shootings. Everyone's voice is needed right now. As a black man from
St. Louis who has done police work in the region, Terrell Carter's voice
is especially needed. I encourage you to read *Walking the Blue Line* and
encourage Terrell to continue his activism, be it the *Ferguson Commission*, to the *Better Together St. Louis* initiative to the *President's Task
Force on 21st Century Policing*. —**Chris King, Managing Editor,** *The
St. Louis American*

The richness of this book is Terrell Carter's capacity to articulate both
the experience of a black male AND a police officer, one who has been
profiled and one who understands the inscribed suspicion necessary
for law enforcement. His perceptive interpretation of the dynamics of
oppression and how forthright conversations can begin, bring balance
to fractured racial perspectives. —**Molly Marshall, Ph.D., President,
Central Baptist Theological Seminary**

Terrell Carter has captured the essence of one of the most pressing issues today—primarily, that significant segments of the communities
have had enough of what they perceive to be harassment in general,
and illegal treatment in particular, by law enforcement personnel and
related agencies. Is it any wonder that the coverage of passionate and
sometimes controversial social unrest continues to dominate local and
international headlines? Mr. Carter's personal experiences give him a

credibility that is truly fascinating. Hopefully many will call upon him to help our communities heal and move forward. —**Sal Martinez, Executive Director of Community Renewal and Development, Community Engagement Expert**

In *Walking the Blue Line*, Terrell Carter shares his experiences as an African-American Christian who has served as a police officer in a volatile urban setting. He is very candid about the frustrations, fears, anger, and sense of alienation he felt during that time, and suggests ways that individual citizens and police authorities can bridge the dangerous separation found in many communities. After reading this book, you will never look at issues of racial division in the same way. —**Ircel Harrison, D.Min., Seminary Professor and Coaching Coordinator, Pinnacle Leadership Associates**

WALKING THE BLUE LINE:

A Police Officer Turned Community Activist
Provides Solutions to the Racial Divide

Terrell L. Carter

B/B
burres books

Bettie Youngs Books Publishing Co. Inc.

www.BettieYoungsBooks.com

Burres Books is an Imprint of Bettie Youngs Books.

If you are unable to order this book from your local bookseller, or online from *Amazon* or *Barnes & Noble,* or from Wholesaler *Baker & Taylor,* or from *Espresso,* or in Braille or Large Print from *Read How You Want,* you may order directly from the publisher: Sales@BettieYoungs.com.

ISBN: 978-1-940784-46-5

Ebook: 978-1-940784-47-2

Library of Congress Cataloging-in-Publication Data: 2015933178

1. Police Officers. 2. Police Brutality. 3. Race Relations. 4. Violence against African-American Youth. 5. Community Policing. 6. Community Engagement. 7. Faith and Employment. 8. Media. 9. Social Activism. 10. Violence Against Youth. 11. Terrell L. Carter. 12. Careers in Law Enforcement. 13. Public Relations.

Contents

Acknowledgements

I want to thank a few of those who helped to bring this book to life. First, I would like to thank publisher Bettie Youngs of Bettie Youngs Book Publishers Co. Inc., and her staff, for giving me the forum to tell this story. To Tatomir Pitariu for the great cover on this book, and to Jazmin Gomez for typesetting and proofing, thank you all so much!

Thank you Derrell Carter, for reviewing the manuscript and providing suggestions on how to tell it more clearly. Thank you Lisette Dennis, for painstakingly editing the manuscript.

Thank you Bryan Guidry of North Broadway Jiu Jets (www.bryanguidrytraining.com) for providing opportunities for me and other Officers to become healthier mentally and physically and relieve some of the tensions that come with the job.

Finally, I would like to acknowledge those who I patrolled the streets with and those who helped to keep me alive: the academy recruits that I graduated with from Class 97-2 and the officers that I worked with in the 3rd, 6th, and 2nd Districts. I think about you and pray for your safety and sanity on a daily basis. I hope for health, protection, and wisdom as you do a job that only a few are capable of doing.

Blessings to you all...

My "Profile:"
A Word from the Author

I am the Executive Director of a community-based service agency that builds affordable housing projects and oversees a number of community-based services for the City of St. Louis. I am also a college professor and program coordinator for a seminary. I am also a board member for multiple service oriented and artistic organizations.

I have earned multiple degrees, among them a Bachelor of Science with a double major in Biblical Studies and Organizational Leadership, a Master of Fine Arts in Arts Management and Leadership, a Doctor of Theology, and I am completing a Doctor of Ministry degree. I have created and taught multiple arts, religion, and interdisciplinary studies at the undergraduate level for some thirteen-plus years.

I've mentored youth and, I am a life and ministry coach. I have served in various capacities of ministry for some twenty-four years. I recognized and accepted my call to ministry when I was 16 years old and began preaching when I was 17.

I am ordained and have served as Minister to Youth, Minister of Administration, Assistant Pastor, and Senior Pastor of historically black churches, as well as racially diverse congregations.

I am an artist; I have exhibited my artwork throughout the United States and overseas. I have won awards for my art and have been profiled about it in print and on television.

I enjoy writing, and am a contributor for two Christian sites, and wrote my first book (Machiavellian Art Management) in 2007.

Best of all, and the "best thing about my life," is my family. I actively participate in my children's lives and make sure they experience a diverse array of things. Like any other loving parent, I make sure to protect, provide, and cherish them at all times.

When I think about my life, I see it as a pretty good "profile" overall. In fact, many friends and associates have called me a "Renaissance Man," and an "upright citizen."

Why is listing all this out significant? Because it is in sharp contrast to the other part of my "profile," namely that if I am pulled over by the police—and the chances of that are good—there is the very real possibility that it won't be because my license plates have expired, or that I was speeding, or had just gone through a stop sign.

My being pulled over will likely be because I'm an African-American male.

In fact, I have regular first-hand experience of being targeted—even harassed—by police, first as a youth because when officers spotted a "brown skinned kid," they automatically assumed that I was up to no good.

And, this happened, still, when I was 20 and I worked as a carpenter's apprentice. After leaving a work site, I was stopped by an officer and told that I "didn't look like I belonged in the area"—in spite of my telling the officer that I'd just left work, and in spite of the fact that my carpentry tools were visible to him in the back seat. Even though visible, he apparently still had a problem: I had to provide the officer with the name of my employer, and, the address of the home that we were remodeling in order to verify that I "did have a reason to be there."

Over the years, I've been stopped because my license plate "did not look right." I've been stopped because my car "did not look like it belonged in the neighborhood." I've been stopped because I looked at the officer in a "strange way" supposedly as I had driven by a police car.

As a 23 year-old police academy recruit for the St. Louis Metropolitan Police Department, I was stopped by an officer from a county municipality who told me he was suspicious of me because I wasn't driving fast enough. Then while talking to me, he noticed that I was wearing my academy issued jacket. A look of shock came over his face when I confirmed that I was an academy recruit for the City of St. Louis. The officer then apologized for stopping me and said, "I hope that you won't make a big deal out of this." Basically, he was worried about me reporting him for racial profiling.

Even now, after all these years of "socially aware" and "social acceptance," and given that I am no longer a kid but rather, in my 40s, I still get pulled over by the police. Like in my youth, I regularly experience the fear of driving through certain areas knowing that I might well be pulled over by law enforcement because they think I just might not belong in the area simply because I'm an African-American male.

These types of experiences are not unique to me, of course.

False assumptions, biases and harassments, happen to black and brown males—each and every day. This is more than unfortunate: it is prejudicial, and, it is damaging.

It's also a bias I understand, because I myself was a police officer who worked in some of the most dangerous neighborhoods in the City of St. Louis.

It is from this distinct and unique combination of experiences from which I offer up my story and, my perspective in working toward effective solutions as we look squarely into the eyes of the racial divide that continues to plague so many.

As such, my overall goal in this book is to neither defend nor demonize police officers, nor to defend or demonize victims of police brutality, but rather, to shed light on how we can understand and repair the strained relationships that all to readily exist within the communities (and especially in minorities) and law enforcement.

To that end, this book is aimed at helping people on the opposing sides of this conversation gain a better understanding of one another so that our communities and the diverse people and police officers within them are not subjected to biases that lead to division, harassment, and brutality. Only then can we make real and productive progress in our race relations. Only then can healing and wholeness be achieved within communities and the officers who serve them.

Foreword

It's a "post-Ferguson" time. This is to say that some of great significance has occurred in the aftermath of the August 9, 2014 shooting and killing of an unarmed 18-year-old black man by a white police officer in the St. Louis suburb of Ferguson, Missouri. As a result the way we look at the racial divide, will never be the same. News of that Saturday night shooting, and the subsequent decision of a grand jury not to charge the police officer, has provoked protest everywhere and a spurred on a new wave of soul-searching about race relations.

In the aftermath of the Ferguson tragedy, underttstanding the racial divide between police and the community will be different. The unanswered question is: Will it be better? Can we learn something that translates into a truer mending of our frayed inter-racial fabric?

Let's hope so.

Author Terrell Carter is uniquely qualified to help us understand the story at the intersection of black and white, someone who has not only a story to tell, but wisdom to go with it and the skill to convey that wisdom in a compelling, practical way. He is:

- An African-American...

- With experience as a police officer...

- In urban St. Louis...

- Whose education has sharpened his critical skills as a perceptive realist...

- Whose faith establishes him in a set of values marked by grace and hope...

- Whose very family gives expression to the idea of blacks and whites living together...

- Whose professional life has been a textbook in reconciliation and collaboration.

It's an impossible set of criteria, right? I would agree were it not for the fact that I know the author of this book personally.

Terrell Carter can speak to this moment in a way few others can. You'll be moved by his story and compelled by the insights he has to share. Read on and see for yourself.

—**Gregory L. Hunt, Ph.D.,** Bestselling and award-winning author of, *Blackbird Singing in the Dead of Night* and *Leading Congregations through Crisis*

Chapter 1
Are Police too Heavy-Handed?

Many of us have seen images of police overstepping their boundaries of authority with individuals from minority groups. From the video of police officers beating Rodney King as he lay on the ground defenseless, to the video of a group of police officers in New York confronting and subduing Eric Garner with a chokehold that led to his death, to a South Carolina police officer shooting an unarmed black man for reaching into his vehicle to retrieve his wallet, the images are startling—yet all too familiar.

The ongoing tense relationship between police and minorities has led to people feeling frustrated and powerless. So many urgent and pressing questions abound.

- What can be done to stop police from regularly harassing—and many times, abusing—people of color?
- What can be done to encourage minorities to want to become law enforcement personnel?
- What can be done to hold law enforcement officials accountable for harming those they have sworn to protect?
- What can be done to change systems that seem to devalue people of color?

These questions and other like them, must be addressed and answered. We must find a way.

Communities worldwide have gone on the offensive to change this landscape. The have protested, marched, conducted "die ins." advocated for the demilitarization of police, mandatory use of body cameras, and pushed for new legislation that would curb some police powers.

Unfortunately, communities have also responded in negative ways, destroying neighborhoods through arson, looting, physical retaliation against officers, and general mayhem.

Like most people who have seen and read stories about police over stepping their boundaries, I have been frustrated and disheartened. I weep for families who lost loved ones by the hands of an officer. I grieve for the officers who have experienced emotional abuse and physical assaults. I weep for fallen officers. I feel frustrated and disheartened at the destruction of property and looting that often occurs within these very communities that have already experienced great losses.

I am disheartened by the erosion of trust between residents and governmental entities that see each other as adversaries, even enemies.

How shall we respond to such emotion evoking events and realities? From Facebook to Twitter to Snapchat to traditional radio call-in shows, there is a diversity of opinions expressed about why minorities and police cannot get along.

The fallout from these types of commentaries and arguments can be dramatic for people on a personal level. Who hasn't heard from a friend promising to never use Facebook again because people had been insensitive towards his or her feelings? Comments are posted by participants on websites classifying groups other than theirs as less than human. We have all heard about family members who no longer associate with each other because they have offended each other to the point of no return.

I have also struggled with how to respond to this racial and cultural divide because of the lens from which I view it: I am African-American male. I am all-too familiar with the racial divide that exists between blacks and whites in our nation and the world. I live in St. Louis, Missouri, and in my opinion, a city with an entrenched history of institutionalized racism.

I have experienced white men yelling expletives at me because I was a black child from North St. Louis who "had no business being in South St. Louis." I have experienced covert racism on multiple job interviews where, other than housekeeping staff, I was the only black person in the building. I have experienced being the only black candidate for a position and being told that I was not qualified for the job because I was "too nice." On another occasion, I was the only black candidate for a job and I was told that I did not get it because I did not "ask enough questions" of the interview committee.

I have first-hand experience both as a youth and an adult of being harassed by police because they thought I was up to no good simply because of the color of my skin. And, their opinions were formed before they found out that I am an upstanding citizen, that in fact for several decades, I was the esteemed Executive Director of a community-based service agency that improves the lives of people in North St. Louis City for 21 years by building affordable housing developments and managing community-based services for the City of St. Louis. Police made their assessment in spite of the fact that I have earned multiple degrees and have taught on the college level and served as a mentor to multiple urban youth, or that I have served in various capacities of ministry for some 24 years.

I understand why they rush to judgment—because I was one of them for five years.

Chapter 2
Life Patrolling the Streets: Are Police Jaded?

Being a police officer was the most stressful and dangerous job that I have ever had. Not having ever dreamed of enforcing the law or protecting people, I became an officer because I needed real employment. I had been praying for a job, one day I heard a radio advertisement for the police force.

At the time I was a 23 year old father-to-be, employed by a small St. Louis company that didn't provide health or retirement benefits. I was desperate for a position that would allow me to take care of my growing family, but without a college degree, my employment prospects were slim.

Due to my negative experiences with police as an adolescent, I initially dismissed the ad. As I thought it through, however, it began to sound like a good idea. A job with the police department represented steady employment and benefits. Also, it would pay my college tuition.

I filled out an application and after three months of interviews, written and physical tests and a psychological evaluation, I was accepted into the police academy. I then began to see the prospect of being a police officer as more than just a job; I saw it as an opportunity to make a difference in the lives of people and communities.

The neighborhood that I had grown up in was not friendly to officers and officers were not friendly to the people living in the neighborhood. Being a policeman, I thought, would position me to help change people's perspective on law enforcement and allow me to positively impact their lives.

However, in the academy I learned that being a police officer was not at all about community service. It was about protecting yourself and your partner; it was about everyday survival on the streets. It sounded both frightening and important at the same time. I graduated—and was assigned to one of the most dangerous districts.

When I started working as a street patrolman, I was scared and unsure. I followed the lead of more experienced officers. I quickly learned that the job was not what I expected or had ever imagined. Suddenly, I realized how woefully unprepared I was emotionally and mentally.

In training I had been taught to assume that anyone who didn't wear blue (the color of our uniforms) could be the enemy and that any citizen could try to take an officer's life, my life. Consequently, no one should be allowed to get within five feet of an officer when you were on a call, the thinking being that if a person were able to get this close to an officer, that person could make a move to harm you before you could respond to defend yourself.

Now a patrolman, I saw this tested many times by drug addicts jumping out of clothes hampers, former professional football players fighting officers because they refused to leave their apartment, and, even grandmothers angered at an officer for writing their grandsons a ticket. People would regularly attempt to put their hands on officers for the purpose of physically harming them. In fact, the graduation motto for my academy class was "If you lose sight of their hands, you lose your life."

While a patrolman, I also realized why you should never let anyone hide his or her hands from you or shift their hands out of sight; they could be hiding a weapon.

The mindset and actions of some officers reflect how they interact with people. They treat them as "other" meaning that "these" people are not a part of their trusted circle and are not worthy of respect. This is evident in the language police officers use: they describe themselves as *good guys* and the people they interact with as *bad guys*. Because of the stress and frustration I felt, I too fell into this practice of seeing citizens as the "other."

Nor did the unspoken department rule of not going against another police officer help this dichotomy. An officer could not question another officer's words or actions in front of someone else. If you did, that officer would feel like you were undercutting him or her and would retaliate. In the street, if a police officer said or did something, you backed him or her up, regardless.

A Sargent drilled this into my head. The first night of working for him, he took me into an interrogation room and told me that I would see some things happen on the street. He said that it would be in my best interest to do what I was told and follow the lead of the more seasoned officers. If I complied and did not cause any problems, I would be okay. This would not be the last time that I was given this specific advice. Shortly thereafter, while in this same squad, I was partnered with a white senior officer to patrol an area known for drug sales. This officer's goal was to help me make a quick arrest in order to build my statistics. We immediately honed in on a man who he believed was selling drugs out of his house.

During our investigation, we found in his home over $1,000 in cash, bags of various unmarked pills and a gun. This could lead to the type of arrest that would make any young officer proud. Except that I wasn't. I didn't think that the man warranted arresting and I could give multiple reasons why.

First, it was not a crime for the man to have $1,000 in cash in his house. During this period, the Internal Revenue Tax returns were being sent out; this man could prove that he and his girlfriend had recently cashed their checks. Also, studies have repeatedly documented that a greater amount of poor urban blacks do not have bank accounts. Instead, they keep their savings at home.

Second, an examination of the pills revealed them to only be over-the-count allergy medicine stored in a plastic sandwich bag, and therefore not either a criminal possession or act.

The gun found was so old and rusted that after holding it, my palms looked like I had been holding mud. The gun was not defaced and the man claimed that it had been his father's. I could not blame him for owning a gun for protection.

The senior officer didn't care about any of the man's explanations. We arrested him and took him into our patrol station. After booking him, the senior officer wrote up the report of what had happened. He then handed it to me and told me to sign it to indicate that I had written it.

Because I had indeed not written it, I balked. Luckily, this happened at the end of our shift and I did not have to decide whether or not to sign at that moment.

Upon leaving the station, I ran into another senior officer with whom I had begun to build a relationship. I told him about the arrest, explained that I didn't feel comfortable signing the report because I didn't believe the man should have been arrested, and asked for his advice. He told me to relax and said he would think it through and suggest how I should handle it at the end of his day. He promised to help me come up with a solution that would not get me into trouble with the other officer and my Sargent.

I went home.

When I arrived at the patrol station for my next shift, the senior officer approached me. He told me that he had heard that I had a problem with how he had handled the previous night's arrest and that I didn't want to sign the police report. In wording not fit to be repeated, he told me that if I ever went behind his back again or questioned something that he had done, I would end up on the streets alone with no protection.

As a rookie with less than six months of street experience, I did what he said and signed the report because I didn't want to make waves with the other officers and didn't want to get on the bad side of any commanding officers to whom he was politically connected. I was certain that I would also need all their help and protection if I ever found myself in a bad situation while patrolling.

After experiencing the daily stress from interacting with the public, not speaking up when I thought an officer had done something wrong to a citizen eventually became all too easy. For example, after being called three times in one day to the same house because of drunken arguments between the husband and wife, I felt like telling them to just get their lives together and leave me alone!

My fellow officers frequently frustrated me and I felt constant disdain for most of the citizens I encountered. In hindsight, these officers and I should have developed adequate coping mechanisms for responding to stress. Also, the department should have advocated regular consultation with counselors or participation in a support group. Healthy outlets to reduce stress should have been identified for officers. Although mental health or coping methods were mentioned in the academy, they were not suggested with police on duty.

In the streets, officers were supposed to be more or less, emotionless: *"You are not a person. You are an extension of the State and the laws that it holds."*

Every aspect about the job had to be controlled and measured.

Art was one of my few healthy outlets. I have drawn and painted since elementary school. During my second year as a Policeman, I was able to exhibit some of my artwork at *Three Sinks Gallery*. For this show, I created multiple, large-scale images that illustrated my frustration with being a police officer.

I painted an image of myself in uniform with slave shackles around my wrists, and titled it "Slave." A chain extended from the shackles to a group of people in the background standing in a vacant urban landscape. The title reflected what I felt like: I was a man with police authority without power or opportunity to make real and positive changes in people's lives.

In another piece I called, In "Everyone's Atlas," I was also featured in uniform. But in this painting I held the earth on my shoulders like the mythological namesake of the work. The work expressed the frustration I felt in being an officer who is expected to help people while remaining anonymous and unacknowledged. Also exhibited in the show was the triptych "Death, Despair, and Damnation." In the paintings I am sitting, with a look of terror on my face and a firearm in hand, on a curb while a dead body is loaded into a medical vehicle. Faceless figures observe. The trio of images represented my fear of possibly shooting someone while on duty.

The show awarded me a small amount of notoriety and positive publicity. But afterwards, I still had to return to work at the same job.

Besides dealing with how to interact with Officers, one of the biggest challenges I encountered was becoming jaded by what I saw and experienced daily. Because our only interactions as officers were with people who lived in a particular community or came from a specific background, they were negative. I realized how difficult it was for the Officers' not to see all these people in the same light. To avoid lumping everyone together, I would need intentional action and continual support from the people who loved me and could be honest with me when they saw a negative change in attitude developing in me.

Admittedly, I was not perfect. While a police officer, I actively practiced my religious faith as a Christian and eventually became pastor of two churches in areas I patrolled. But I'm sure that some people I encountered during my time with the police department would have questioned my salvation. But to be honest, in general, no one I ran into on the streets cared about my religious activities and the Department would not have appreciated me talking about it to citizens. This didn't prevent me from trying to incorporate principles of my faith into my work, however.

I tried regularly to be kind and understanding. Often people perceived my display of compassion as a sign of weakness and would try to take advantage of me. Then I was forced to respond in an appropriate manner. Sometimes I spoke slowly, softly and clearly. But other times to assert control, I screamed and shouted over someone who was doing the same. They would then follow my commands!

Another challenge for me as an officer was the fact that I was not being called on when things were going well. I was only called when situations had gotten really bad. I was not called at the beginning of the dispute. My job was to show up when a response was needed. Consequently, I was constantly on guard due to not knowing fully what I was walking into when I arrived on a scene.

Working in this environment demanded that I view every situation or person as something to respond to and fix. Then I could move on to the next circumstance that required remediation. I struggled to remember that all people, including me, are broken and needed God's grace. It took effort to remember that just because a person was experiencing tough times didn't make that person "bad." Perhaps he or she may have simply made a poor decision, or, someone else's decision had affected him or her drastically, the circumstances under which I was meeting them was not necessarily an accurate depiction of what type of person they were.

Since I strived to show people an appropriate amount of grace; life patrolling the streets was a tough balancing act. I wanted to see citizens as more than just people complaining, people who needed to learn proper communication and parenting skills or people who needed to learn how to manage their liquor or life. But as soon as I would let my guard down, someone would test me and try to take advantage of me—both emotionally and physically.

As a believer of God's grace, I appreciated my Faith over the concept of law and pursued living it out in my actions as an officer. Not always successful, I remained aware that people were not necessarily bad or unworthy of God's love even when they did something that required law enforcement's involvement. However, experience taught me to be aware of the need to protect others and myself, even when I was helping. Returning home every day at the end of my shift was my most important goal.

Despite my desire to help others, some citizens made clear that they did not care about me either as an officer or as a person. Nor did they care that I was interim pastor in a neighborhood church, mentor to urban youth, artist or father. They saw the uniform and had a preconceived idea of who I was and what I could do for them. They would also respond to me, and other officers, in dangerous ways. On multiple occasions, I helped officers defend themselves against people who trying to hurt them physically.

This was my life for almost five years. This is what I ate and breathed until, according to my plan, I would work as a policeman for five years and then quit. It was time for me to finish my undergraduate and graduate degrees. Then, at 28, I could find less stressful and better-paid employment.

Chapter 3
Racial Profiling—Does it Work?

Minorities often complain that law enforcement regularly practice racial profiling. But what is racial profiling, and why do police officers engage in it, and what criteria do they use when they apply it?

In "A Resource Guide on Racial Profiling Data Collection Systems: Promising Practices and Lessons Learned," authors Deborah Ramirez, Jack McDevitt and Amy Farrell clearly define racial profiling, saying that "Any police-initiated action that relies on the race, ethnicity or national origin rather than the behavior of an individual or information that leads the police to a particular individual who has been identified as being, or having been, engaged in criminal activity" is what it is. I agree with them.

As a young officer, I was taught that profiling was a useful and necessary tool whose application assisted police in conducting investigations. Racial profiling began with examining a person's or thing's "fit." If the "fit" was wrong or inconsistent, then it would warrant investigation. For example if a car doesn't "fit" in a neighborhood, it might be stolen.

While on patrol, if I spotted a brand new Mercedes Benz in a neighborhood where the majority of residents lived below poverty, red flags would go off. Typically, a high-ticket car is not consistent with this type of neighborhood. Also, if a driver doesn't look he "fits" the car being driven, then he may need to be investigated. A preteen male driving a brand new Mercedes Benz would send up a red flag. Although the male may fit the neighborhood, the driver did not fit the car.

This procedure's application was not limited to black people. If I spotted a white person while patrolling a black neighborhood, I would also question his or her "fit." It wasn't that white people were not allowed in black communities, but I would question whether this particular person fit in the one that I was patrolling. Did that white person look or act anxious? Did he or she act like they were lost? Did the person look like he or she was on a mission to get somewhere, or, were they relaxed and comfortable in their surroundings?

The subsequent investigation results differed. On one occasion, after having followed for several blocks, I stopped an older white man who was driving very slowly through a black neighborhood. I suspected that he might have been looking for drugs or a prostitute. I was wrong. He was a pastor, and after visiting a parishioner, had gotten lost driving down the unfamiliar streets.

On another night, I spotted a bad fit: a white motorcyclist crashed in a black neighborhood. Upon interrogation, the driver admitted to purchasing drugs, cheating the dealers and tried to speed away.

So those are various situations in which "profiling" is used as a matter of applying "common sense." There is no malice, just a "Does what I'm seeing *fit*?"

Ideally, profiling would never be a simple, straight forward process based only on a person's skin color. Multiple factors would feed an officer's assumptions and actions, and the subsequent investigation.

In "Racial Profiling Studies in Law Enforcement: Issues and Methodology" author Jim Cleary posits two distinct definitions of racial profiling: narrow and broad. He writes "under the narrow definition, racial profiling occurs when a police officer stops, questions, arrests and/or searches someone solely on the basis of the person's race or ethnicity," and under the broad definition, "racial profiling occurs whenever police routinely use race as a factor that, along with an accumulation of other factors, causes an officer to react with suspicion and take action." The later suggests that racial profiling has the potential to be a positive tool to assist officers in solving, managing, or deterring crime during an investigation of something or someone.

Racial profiling is not a twenty-first or twentieth century phenomenon. Robert Staples provides a brief history in "White Power, Black Crime, and Racial Politics," saying that as early as 1693, court officials in Philadelphia authorized the police to "take up any 'Negro' seen 'gadding about' without a pass from his or her master." This judiciary order to stop and arrest any black found on the street made no distinction between free and slave blacks. In fact, the Black Codes of the Southern region allowed militiamen to arrest and detain blacks whose presence aroused suspicion. The Fugitive Slave Act of 1850 threatened both law enforcement officials and ordinary citizens with severe fines if they failed to assist in the capture of suspected runaway slaves, particularly when the suspicion could be based only on written claims: "free and enslaved blacks did not have the right to defend themselves in court against such claims." Racial profiling has its roots in the slave-owners controlling their so-called property.

Though the Civil Rights Act of 1964 aims to reduce the possibility that entire racial groups could be, law enforcement can still legally target individuals based on race. In fact, Supreme Court decisions rule that police can stop people because of their membership in a particular ethnic group, as long as the police provide some additional reason for the stop, such as a "hunch."

People think that the police do just randomly stop people of color. They are, in my opinion, both right and wrong.

Here's how they are wrong. Police officers spend most of their time responding to citizen tips and complaints called in to 911. When a person calls, the complaint or information about a crime is dispatched to a patrol car assigned to the area of the incident. At that moment the officer must investigate.

Callers may give only a general description of the incident or people involved. For example, someone reports that a "suspicious" black man was selling drugs at the corner of Grand at Arsenal. The officer, lacking details, does not know what the black man is wearing, whether he is in a vehicle or on foot or if he is alone. This occurred so frequently that one of my black partners and I would turn to each other and jokingly ask, "What did you do?"

The point is, the investigating officer, and ultimately those under scrutiny, would benefit more if citizens provided complete and accurate information.

Here's how citizens are right when they say officers harass them.

Unfortunately, some police officers will pursue people to harass and arrest. Multiple reasons lie behind this behavior. An officer's career is based on statistics (stats). They are rewarded for compiling stats related to arrests, especially drug arrests. They are not rewarded for being "Officer Friendly" who helped people and families work through personal issues and improve communication.

Higher stats numbers result in better treatment by commanding officers, and increased possibility of promotion or a transfer to a more desirable work assignment. To become an officer who is valued by superiors, he or she has to make arrests for a variety of crimes and make sure that those arrested spend time in jail or prison.

We were reminded regularly that our job was to respond to calls and write tickets, and this would serve as evidence of our work for the District Captain. In short, what this means is that Officers often profile and arrest to improve their career.

Also, people who are "easy targets" are profiled. Often, we are conditioned us to distrust and fear black men. How many of us could admit to feelings of fear and distrust upon seeing a black male who looks like he stepped off a hip hop video set. If he is wearing sagging pants, has a gold tooth and unkempt hair or a baseball cap, we might assume he is a thug. Police realize this. Consequently, when their stats need to be increased, Police often arrest the person that most people don't trust or care about. Sad but true.

In the article "What Power, Black Crime, and Racial Politics," Robert Staples writes, "Given the millions of ordinary Americans who violate some law, it is not practical to jail all offenders. What is unfair is that the criminal justice system does not imprison the people who represent the greatest threat to the society; it jails primarily the poor and the powerless. Contrary to conventional wisdom, the seriousness of a crime is not the most crucial element in predicting who goes to prison and who does not. About two-thirds of the people in state prisons and municipal jails are black and Latino, who tend to be poorer and less educated than the typical white collar criminal."

"Arrest rates," says Staples, "are three to four times higher for blacks than for whites, when black Americans are less likely than whites to use most drugs, and there is no credible evidence that they sell drugs more often. Blacks are arrested more often simply because police selectively target the drugs black people sell and the areas in which they sell them."

In the end, the reason an officer arrests someone really doesn't matter. What does matter is that the officer has the "magic pen." Officers know that ultimately, what is written in a report will more than likely be accepted and believed because that officer controls the information that the prosecuting attorney and public will see.

If I stop a person for littering and he does something to anger me or doesn't follow orders, I can say that he attempted to assault me. No one will know that he didn't. It is my word against his and a police officer's word carries more weight than the person being cited.

So, while profiling to assist in legitimate investigation can be a valuable tool to fight crime and support neighborhoods, when it is used to make arrests to build an officer's resume, it is wrong. And, it is destructive. It destroys lives.

Chapter 4
Why Police Officers Never Snitch on One Another

As an officer, I did think the "group think." Intentional REthinking, regular prayer and encouragement from my friends, professionals and family members, eventually helped me to begin stop seeing everyone as so-called "villains." This change was not easy and did not happen overnight. As time passed though, I was able to have a better attitude toward the people I served.

I worked on improving the relationships with the people I came into contact with on the streets. But I didn't enjoy the job more. Instead, my disdain continued to grow and reinforce my desire to leave. I was becoming someone I didn't want to be, and no doubt, someone God did not want me to be. My life was under constant stress and I worried continually about protecting my loved ones and myself.

Witnessing racial profiling was disturbing and stressful, as well. As I recall my experiences, I find it incredulous that people in law enforcement honestly believe and say that a racial divide and racial profiling doesn't exist. An officer's mind is divided: first, between the police and the general public and second, between the police and minorities.

Whenever a black or brown male lacked valid reasons for being in certain places or for driving certain vehicles at certain times of day, profiling was guaranteed. Officers assumed these men were criminals. Wearing specific clothes, listening to a specific kind of music and consorting with a specific type of person meant that they were up to no good. Without a doubt, many good and Godly people have had their lives adversely affected because only their clothes and location informed an officer's judgment.

My anger at citizens morphed into anger with police officers. Police officers were disproportionately profiling black people. Although some of the racial profiling was prompted by calls from concerned citizens and the desire and need to secure easy stats, it was greatly generated from seeing black people as "other."

I regularly confronted the dilemma of keeping quiet about what I heard and saw or reporting an offending officer's actions to a supervisor. I never reported them because I knew that if it were found out that I had snitched, I would be a pariah. If I were ever in trouble on the street with a suspect and needed that officers help, I would not receive it. The majority of white officers would no longer trust me. I would be alone.

This rang true too with black officers, as well. The ultimate police commandment is to absolutely avoid getting another officer into trouble. In my situation, if I brought suspicion and accusations onto any officers, it would sound the death knell for my family members and me. I had a black son, three black brothers, and a black nephew who could all be targets if I made the wrong person or people in the department angry. In what way would my loved ones be targeted? The possibility was beyond comprehension.

My frustration with the pursuit of stats and profiling grew while my planned resignation approached. An arrest by one of my former partners brought everything to a head.

I was assigned, with a senior black officer, to work a coveted under-cover detail. Listed as Public Affairs Officers, we usually did not wear police uniforms. Supplied with an unmarked car, we worked Monday through Friday from 8 a.m. until 4 p.m. Officially, our job was to serve as liaisons between the department and the community to improve relationships. We were given a tremendous amount of flexibility.

My partner was highly decorated and cared about the community he served. In black neighborhoods, he had regularly participated in and led marches seeking to end violence and the sales of illegal drugs. This officer called dealers "terrorists who were ruining our community." A boxing and basketball coach, he mentored children. His own children played on the neighborhood teams that he coached. I admired that he wanted to make a difference in people's lives.

Our first day together, I learned that our real job duties were to conduct surveillance on suspected drug dealers and execute search warrants in expectation of finding narcotics and illegal contraband. On my first day working in that position, our black commanding officer told me that I would be fine if I followed the senior officer's lead and did what I was told. Again, these words would serve as an omen of the things to come.

Despite all the good things I had learned about my partner, I soon realized that he was also aggressive and stat driven. He had worked in multiple specialized units, had been awarded Officer of the Year and now wanted to be sergeant.

Initially, our partnership functioned well. I was eager to learn investigative techniques and my partner was able and willing to share the tricks of the trade.

The regular schedule was ideal for both of us. I could raise my son and finish my graduate degree. No commanding officers harassed us as long as we proved we were working to get serious leads on drug dealers. I had an added impetus to clean up the neighborhood: our surveillance area was near the church where my paternal grandfather served as pastor.

Unfortunately, our working relationship did sour. His aggressive treatment towards people, I felt, was deplorable. I did not like how he saw most young black men as destructive "terrorists." That he had anointed himself judge and jury frustrated me. I was once again stuck in a situation that I could not see a way out of because he was well connected to the leaders of the police department. Standing up to him would mean that I was putting my future in harm's way.

One day I found myself again in a no-win situation. My partner and I had legitimately arrested several people on drug related crimes. The report my partner wrote, however, was filled with lies.

What actually happened was that at the beginning of our shift, a detective informed us that a woman was holding drugs. Employed at a

Christian daycare, she was apparently waiting until her ex-boyfriend, a known dealer, would retrieve them and pay her for holding onto them. We went to the daycare to question the woman. Eventually, she admitted to possessing the drugs and was arrested.

During the investigation, my partner told me that he had been trying to catch this dealer for multiple years without any luck. This was his opportunity to finally arrest him.

Eventually, the drug dealer arrived at the daycare to pick up his package. We arrested him and two people accompanying him. None of these people were angels. All but one (the woman hiding the drugs) had been previously convicted of multiple crimes.

After the arrests, my partner wrote a report comprised of fabrications. In it, he lied about how we learned about the drugs, how the drugs were found, who possessed the drugs and how the suspects were arrested. I was not required to read or approve the report. As the arresting officer, he handled preparing it and taking it through the department's chain of command. He submitted it for approval by the commanding officers. Then, it was sent to federal prosecutors to ensure that those arrested would face federal prison instead of a shorter time in a state prison facility.

Later on, I did receive a copy and realized it was a resounding lie. However, if I did not go along with what he had written, I would be the target of retaliation. My conscious would not let me rest. I debated whether I would go along with what I had been taught were the department's methods or would I do what was right.

Several weeks later, federal prosecutors contacted me. They invited me to a meeting to discuss the report. I told them that the report did not reflect what I remembered. With those words, I crossed the line and could not backtrack. Furthermore, when word got back to my fellow officers that I had told the truth and gone against my partner, I would need to resign immediately and prepare to protect my family and myself, by any means necessary.

The federal government launched an investigation into whether my partner had violated the civil rights of the people arrested. They told me that a separate investigation had been already been opened related to my partner due to multiple past complaints against him. A long list of people claimed that my partner had falsely arrested them and stolen their property.

A trial eventually ensued and my partner was convicted of multiple charges. Ironically, all of the people who my partner arrested and lied about, were black.

I didn't emerge from the investigation squeaky-clean. During my initial conversation with the federal prosecutors, I volunteered to tell them that I had struck one of the arrested men.

During the arrests, one of the accomplices had refused to get out of their car, so I had to wrestle him out. After handcuffing the man, I quickly searched him but found nothing. I put him into the rear of our unmarked police car. Then, I noticed him moving around a lot. After pulling him out of the car, I searched it. He had slid a loaded revolver beneath the backseat. In hastily frisking him, I had earlier missed the weapon he had hidden in his pants.

Fear and rage rose up in me as I have never experienced before. I could have been killed. Suddenly, my mortality was very real. Because I hadn't properly searched this suspect he could have shot me. A handful of drugs could have cost me my life. While taking this man into custody, I repeatedly punched him with my fists. I couldn't stop swinging, or crying. All I could think about was that I had almost been taken away from my young son.

I also remembered that a suspect had killed an officer less than a year prior. The arresting policeman had failed to thoroughly search the man before putting him in the rear of the patrol car. Having hidden a gun in his pants, the suspect retrieved that gun and shot through the window and killed the officer.

The prosecutors did not approve of my having punched the suspect; but they understood. As the investigation progressed, I hired a lawyer to negotiate immunity for me. Because I had done wrong, I struggled with receiving immunity. But I didn't want to go to jail for assaulting someone who could have easily killed me. I continue to struggle with my actions and decisions.

In the end, my partner was convicted and sentenced to serve federal time.

And I quit the police force.

Chapter 5
Why Police Officers Always Seem "Angry"

Prior to my partner's dubious arrests, I had already wanted to resign from the police department. Police work was physically, mentally and spiritually draining. I was no longer happy-go-lucky. Instead, I was a hardened, cranky man in blue.

I did not appreciate the people I was charged with protecting, and conversely, I knew they did not appreciate me. Because citizens only welcomed police officers when there was a problem, I didn't feel motivated to go to work. People only cared about what they wanted an officer to do right then and there. Regularly, I was told, "I pay your taxes, so you work for me!" This is the wrong thing to say to an officer.

The stress was never ending. Paid less than $38,000 a year, I also worked multiple part-time jobs in security while raising my son and completing a graduate degree.

As a police officer, I witnessed a lot of crime and pain on a daily basis; I became hyper-sensitive to everyone and everything around me. I was always vigilant about my family and my safety. I feared retribution from people who were not pleased with what occurred when I was on duty. It was tough to distance myself from being identified with my role as an Officer of the law since I lived in the city and often ran into people I had encountered on duty.

One day my twin brother, who was not a policeman, called. The nervousness in his voice scared me. He and his family were in a store when two men walked in. They stopped dead upon seeing my brother. He overheard them saying that they recognized him from the streets as

Officer Carter. My brother said that they left and returned to their car where they either put something in or took something out. I urged him to gather his family and leave instantly. Luckily, nothing happened.

My duty as an officer was to protect others and not myself. I could not ignore or escape a fight or shooting. Instead I was obliged to run to it to contain or stop it.

Stores and restaurants welcomed on and off duty police officers. When something went wrong, we were expected to fix it. Because I was obliged to talk to or walk out belligerent customers, I always carried my gun and a set of handcuffs. I had taken an oath to protect and serve in or out of uniform.

I soon grew weary of sacrificing my personal, and, individual identity. While on the job, I was no longer a person, but instead I was the embodiment of the law. I didn't have any individual rights. When someone fought me, he was not fighting Terrell. He was fighting the city and state laws.

When people found out that I was an officer, this fact helped to squash their racist thoughts and treatment towards me. As a black man, storeowners regularly shadowed me, suspecting that I would try to steal merchandise. But when I paid, they often spotted my badge and their attitudes changed. Then, they expressed gratitude for police officers and invited me to return again to shop.

On multiple occasions I remember walking in certain areas of south St. Louis business districts. Inevitably, if I walked too close to any middle-aged or older white woman, they would clutch their purses and cross the street so I would not be near them. I eventually got tired of this happening and began to approach the people, show them my badge and tell them that if anyone did try to rob or harm them, they could feel comforted knowing that I was in the vicinity to help and protect.

As a result of my frustrations, I soon began to feel a sense of entitlement. If I had to deal with all their problems and had to sacrifice my safety and well-being, then they "owed me." I was, after all, one who helped keep things under control.

I was suspicious of everyone but my family. I felt like most people were criminals. Every single mother looked the same and had the same problems. Young men who did not graduate from high school, shared similar unredeemable characteristics.

I was angry because people couldn't take care of their own problems. It was a cycle. I knew that during the spring, I would be called to one particular home because the father's job was seasonal and he spent his downtime drinking which led to problems with his wife. During the summer, this particular family would regularly fight and then call police. During the winter, a different family would fight and then call police.

I was angry because people would call 911 for the smallest things, including, but not limited to requests for police officers to come to a home so they could scare a child who was not behaving for their parent.

I was angry because the job was not concerned with how to help people but to go from call to call and help people to understand why they should not call 911 for all of their problems.

I was angry because the job was stat driven and not people driven.

All of this anger eventually led to me becoming a different person—a person who I did not like being. As different as it is to admit, while on duty, I looked forward to potentially fighting citizens who tried to push the boundaries because it became an outlet to release my anger and frustration.

All of this fueled my resignation and I bid law enforcement farewell —and resumed my activism within my community in new and more productive ways.

But my service to the community that I previously patrolled would not end there.

Chapter 6
Community Activism—as a Pastor

Several months after leaving the police department, I became the pastor of the Broadway Baptist Church. It was located in the area where I experienced the most frustration as a policeman. Vacant lots and derelict housing were the norm in this severely blighted, depressed and poor neighborhood. Crime and drugs ran rampant. Prostitutes worked the sidewalk in front of the church. While on the force, I would periodically sit, and write reports, in the church's parking lot—mostly to intimidate would-be criminals.

The former pastor, an older white man, led a young black male to a confession of faith and baptism. But one day they met in the church basement and the young man struck the pastor in the head with a coffee urn. After stealing the pastor's wallet and keys, he fled. The pastor's wife and a police officer discovered the pastor who later died from his injuries. The murderer was arrested and imprisoned.

The church struggled to keep members and securing another spiritual leader. Who would want to lead a dwindling congregation? Who would want to minister a church whose pastor was murdered by a parishioner?

Apparently, God thought that I did.

An acquaintance, knowledgeable about my desire to serve and my familiarity with the neighborhood, contacted me. He recommended I send Broadway Baptist Church my resume. I did and was invited to speak at a morning service.

Seven white members greeted me upon my arrival at the church. The youngest was in her late 50s, the others were in their 70s. I questioned whether I was at the right place. That first service went well and they asked me back. Within a month, they invited me to serve as their pastor. I accepted.

Admittedly, this was not my idea of the first church that I would lead. In Bible College and seminary, I prepared myself to lead a well-off congregation. But this was not God's plan.

For a year, the congregation remained small. We lost two members due to their failing health and advancing age which prevented them from driving to Service. However, neighborhood people, prostitutes and prison parolees involved in a Christian rehabilitation program all began to attend. I was initially surprised and cautious when interacting with those that I had encountered while I was a police officer. But I continued to serve. My family members and old friends with their families joined. The congregation grew in size and Outreach. The church maintained vital ministries that weekly provided clothing and food to neighborhood residents.

I was proud that the church welcomed everyone. We invited a group of 15 adults with severe disabilities and developmental disorders to worship with us. We found ways to accommodate their desire to be active. They formed a choir and helped lead services every other Sunday.

This was our opportunity to imitate God's unconditional love. One disabled girl's mother pulled me aside and told me that she hadn't known churches to welcome "everyone," regardless of mental illness or physical disability. She didn't know that Churches like ours existed. The significance of our Church and its outreach and mission to serve "all," amazed me, too.

Those experiences continue to inform my thoughts on how to treat people. Broadway Baptist Church parishioners reminded me that everyone deserves to have his or her worth recognized and affirmed. All God's children should be welcomed, whether we consider them worthy or not. We are not to judge.

After five years, my service with that congregation ended and I left, hopefully having grown in wisdom and love.

Chapter 7:
Navigating the Police-Community Racial Divide: Suggestions to Help Restore Trust within Communities

How do we navigate the challenges of protecting and serving our communities? How can we move forward?

I don't agree with or justify all actions or attitudes of officers (nor the protocol of Police Departments), but I can understand why they respond the way they do under certain circumstances. As a black man who has been harassed by police, as well as beyond frustrated myself when dealing with citizens breaking laws, I do understand the frustration that citizens feel when dealing with officers who act like they do not want to help people and treat people like they are "other."

But, because of my experiences as an officer, I know that all officers are not thugs who don't like juveniles, minorities or black men in particular. That being said, I would like to offer some suggestions that I believe will help police officers and the communities they serve as we all try to find ways to live together and work together for the greater good of all.

✓　**Invest in a process that seeks to help officers cope with the stresses of the job.** Departments should make professional counseling a mandatory part of police life. During my tenure on the job, the only time that mental health was discussed was during the Academy. During my five years of patrolling streets and interacting with people, I was not encouraged to talk to anyone about anything that I experienced while on patrol. Instead, the attitude was that I should get used to seeing gruesome things happen on a regular basis as a part of the job.

I regularly responded to suicides, shootings, and stabbings. I was never asked if I needed to talk to a mental health professional after I investigated someone's death. Yes, Police Officers constantly see fatal injuries and brutality among the masses, but it doesn't mean they are immune from the emotional duress of it.

Although I experienced horrific things multiple times, I cannot adequately describe what it is like to see someone die before your eyes from being stabbed, shot, or, physically run over by a vehicle. I cannot put into words what it feels like to have to knock on a family's door and tell a family that they will never see a loved one alive again. I cannot convey the hurt and anger I felt after helping a child who was physically or sexually abused.

I would have benefitted from going to a counselor. Instead, I did what more experienced officers did: tried to put it out of my mind. While it seemed to me that while some officers become jaded to what they see, I know that I will carry these memories for the rest of my life. I can only imagine what officers who have worked for 20 years or more have experienced and subsequently, suppressed in order to consistently do their job.

✓ **Police departments should work to counteract the negative stigmas that are placed on officers who do eventually feel burned out by all they experience.** Officers are taught that in their work, they are not to think of themselves as a person as much as "an extension of the law." Officers have to be at peak performance, tough, and strong, at all times. But this does not mean that they are not empathic nor immune from emotional duress or pain. In fact, opinions polls show that some officers feel like they have little hope in their lives, and in fact, police and other officers of the law have some of the highest suicide and divorce rates.

If officers felt more supported by their departments and co-workers, it could lead to better health and longer lives for some of them. This could start with departments sponsoring support groups for them and their family members. I mention family members because officers do not do their jobs alone. Whenever they are on duty, spouses and other family members are hoping that that officer—a husband, father, brother, son and so on, comes home safe and sound.

✓ **Police Departments must create an enviroment that makes it safe for other officers who commit crimes.** Not every policeman approves of what other officers do. But, if they do not think that they will be protected when they do come forward and report something, they never will. I eventually testified against my partner, but I knew that I had to leave the department in order to protect myself against retaliation from other officers. Years later, there is still a negative stigma about me with some people in the department because I told the truth about an incident wherein some of the facts were falsified.

People wonder why I never reported any of the misdeeds that I witnessed to the Internal Affairs Division. I did not because Internal Affairs, like any other division in a law enforcement agency, is made up of other police officers. The St. Louis City department was small enough that most officers knew each other. If I would have reported an incident, it was likely that officer would know about it before the day was over. He or she could then come up with a plan or story to make me out to be a liar and no one would take my side, because Officers were never supposed to get another officer into trouble.

✓ **Law Enforcement Agencies can stop rewarding officers for only working toward getting big statistics in certain categories.** Consistently, Officer-of-the-Year awards are given for drug busts and successful search warrants. It is very rare for officers to be acknowledged, let alone rewarded with promotion or transfers to choice specialized units, for doing community-based "good deeds," including working toward the visibility that allowed officers to be seen in the community as "good guys." Officers who want to be promoted, and move up in rank and influence, will gravitate to doing the things that get them noticed by a Superior, which usually includes some type of high profile arrest.

✓   **Citizen on Patrol Academy or, a Citizen's Police Academy, should be offered on a consistent basis.** This would give departments an opportunity to meet and interact with citizens in an environment that is not stressful and combative, which is typically how citizens and officers interact. That Police be seen by the community in congenial situations goes a long way to improving the community's perception of Police as being *important* to all citizens in a community. It can alleviate fear and hate of officers, and promote goodwill.

✓   **Political officials and department commanders should invite regular everyday people from within the community to serve in community-based-leadership positions (instead of political appointees who are being rewarded for supporting politicians during election seasons).** When a person is appointed to a Citizen Review Board or Police Commission by a Mayor or Governor, citizens know that their best interests will not be served. The only primary interests served will be those of the person who has been nominated.

✓   **Police departments need to add cultural sensitivity training to their requirements for officers on the street (as well as for those in the academy.)** I patrolled the streets with white officers who did not understand anything about black culture and had misgivings about most all of the blacks they encountered on the job. Interestingly, many of these white police officers literally had few if any black friends or acquaintances, other than fellow officers. Black Officers were not surprised, because white officers always saw black people at their worst.

This suggestion can help all cultures better understand each other. For example, as a young officer, I responded to a call for service at the home of a Korean family. When I arrived, the mother opened the door. I immediately began to ask her questions. She shied away from me and began to point me to her husband. I continued to ask her questions and she continued to defer to her husband. I finally engaged the man, but he responded to me in disdain.

What I eventually learned was that I had violated the social norms of their culture. I should not have spoken to the mother first. I should have acknowledged her presence but then, as a sign of respect and recognition of his position as head of his household, spoke to the father first. Ignorant of cultural norms within the Korean family, the woman's husband saw my actions as a sign of disrespect.

I had multiple experiences like this. I learned the hard way that different cultures communicated in certain ways and, that their natural cultural tendencies were vastly different from what I was used to.

I can't say that I was aware of all this when I first began to patrol the streets. When I initially experienced these cultural intricacies, I thought they were challenging me and the authority of the badge. In actuality, they were being themselves.

Some type of training that makes officers aware of these cultural differences would help officers better understand those they serve.

It is not only the responsibility of police to improve relations with community members, but as well, the citizens who will inevitably interact with police at some point in their lives. To that end, the suggestions are useful.

✓ **Every citizen who is concerned about how officers do their job, should attend a local police department's Citizen on Patrol Academy or Citizens Police Academy.** During these academies, citizens are given a glimpse into situations such as what it is like to be a police officer, how a 911 call is dispatched, and how an investigation is conducted, and so on.

Attending one of these types of training sessions would give citizens a bird's eye view into how they can help officers do their jobs and help their communities. Citizens can learn what laws are relevant to their city. They can learn the rights and responsibilities of citizens and law enforcement. And more.

I would also recommend that if possible, citizens participate in a ride along with a police officer. There is nothing like hearing and seeing a situation from a patrol car and an officer's point of view. For even the avergage citizen, it's an eye-opener and can go a long way toward improving Police/Community relationships.

✓ **Citizens can volunteer to participate in, or seek to be elected to, their local police department's Citizen Review Board.** Service on this type of board is not simply to try to hold officers accountable for their actions, as much as an opportunity to hold citizens accountable for their actions when interacting with officers and other people from within the community. Through Citizen Review Boards, people can learn all sides of a situation, which in turns can improve the relationships of all concerned.

✓ **Citizens can participate in a local Neighborhood Ownership Model Plan (NOM).** A NOM plan is a flexible community-based approach to creating and implementing ideas that lead to significant and lasting crime reduction in neighborhoods. It is volunteer driven and incorporates cooperation from various city departments. A NOM plan consists of the following aspects:

- A Neighborhood Planning Team that leads the efforts to create and implement the plan;
- Citizen Patrol Units that are made up of residents who volunteer to patrol streets in order to record and report crime;
- Regular Community Meetings that are organized by neighbors in order to provide education, information and facilitate interaction between government agencies and the community; and,
- Neighborhood Victim Support Teams made up of trained neighbors who help victims of crimes to ensure they have the support they need to manage through the legal system and the emotional upheaval that follows.

More information about creating and implementing a NOM plan

can be found at http://www.circuitattorney.org/NeighborhoodOwner-shipModel.aspx.

✓   **All citizens should become familiar with the various city departments that serve the needs of people in their neighborhoods.** For example, the Neighborhood Stabilization Officer (NSO) or Neighborhood Improvement Specialist (NIS) is primarily responsible for helping citizens, and citizen groups, identify solutions to neighborhood problems. The scope of their services varies from the typical (making sure trash is picked up in a timely manner) to bigger concerns (such as getting a derelict building demolished). A NSO/NIS is an invaluable resource for any community.

✓   **Every family bears the responsibility to teach their children how to properly interact with law enforcement.** We should teach our children that officers do have a certain level of authority at all times. When a policeman gives a person an appropriate legal command, that command should be followed, not challenged. When someone defies an appropriate legal command, he or she has started the process of the escalation of force, and the officer is then obliged and/or expected to use a level of force that is appropriate to get the citizen to follow his or her commands.

Notice that I said, "appropriate legal command" and "appropriate level of force." Officers who do not follow the legal parameters that are set for them should be held subject to punishment, as any other citizen would.

✓   **Parents should also teach their children that when an Officer is present, to always keep their hands where an officer can see them.** If someone hides his or her hands, whether on purpose or accident, an officer will immediately think that person is reaching for something to cause harm to the Officer. Unfortunately, this is the nature of the beast. Too many officers have been harmed when a person was able to reach into his or her pocket or under the seat, and retrieve a knife or gun.

✓   **We all must acknowledge and deal with the fact that much of the crime and killings that are perpetrated on the black community are committed by black people, not police officers.** Yes, police officers have killed unarmed black people. This is never acceptable. Officers must be held accountable and justice must be found for victims of police abuse.

But, the point is, it is easier to call out a white officer who treated me poorly than to publicly criticize a young black child from my own neighborhood who regularly breaks into cars. Statistics show that black males kill other black males at a disproportionately higher rate than anyone else. Sad but true—and something *must* be done about it.

As a community, we must address the fact that black and brown children do actually commit crimes and our communities suffer because of this. This is something that our communities must get honest about and find solutions as to why this is so.

✓   **As much as law enforcement and the citizenry need to take responsibility for their parts in the divide that exists between police and communities, the media also has to acknowledge the part they play in building (or eroding) the goodwill between the police and their respective communities.** For starters, I appreciate those who report the news and oftentimes find themselves in harm's way in reporting the events of the day. But the media, known for their "if it bleeds it leads" mentality, must be willing to become a part of the solution too, meaning that it would be advantageous if they would report the "do-gooding" of police, in other words, police officers doing good things for people within their respective communities. It is also important for the media to showcase citizens who report on the good that came of things because of police intervention, and so on.

In my opinion, it sometimes seem that the media is biased about some things, and presents that bias in their reporting—as opposed to simply providing accurate information about a person or incident, and letting it stand.

In the rush to be the first on the scene, or to get the first sound bite, or to capture a dramatic image, media may move with less care than usual, sometimes giving incorrect information, or engage in reporting that doesn't give the full information in order for the community to assimilate the incident without themselves becoming biased. This ultimately hurts everyone and only serves to spur on the division between police and the community. How unfortunate. The Society of Professional Journalists has been in existence since 1909 with the purpose of "protecting and improving journalism." In fact they are to:

- seek the truth and report it;
- minimize harm; and,
- be accountable and transparent.

There must be a return to that standard of excellence if the media is to do their part in aiding the way we each view events—and one another.

Hopefully the media will want to help restore trust between police and communities and this will be reflected in their reporting. As media outlets seek to report clearly and accurately, we can have more transparent conversations about the real issues—which can better lead to solutions so as to lessen the existing tension and divide.

There are other ways we can move toward peaceful resolution, and I invite you to be a part of the solution.

Where Do We Go from Here?

The year 2014 may serve as an important year in the story of police and community relations. Many incidents occurred that brought the world's attention to issues that the black community had been trumpeting for several years.

As we all move forward in these discussions, a question remains: "What's next?" How do we learn from everything that has happened? How can we learn from the decisions and actions made by people like the Mayor and Police Chief of Ferguson, the Police Chief of St. Louis County, and the Governor of Missouri in the wake of the Michael Brown shooting? What can we learn from the protests that occurred throughout college campuses and streets of various cities?

Amid corporate fear and personal struggle to answer the "what next" question, I offer my hopes for the type of leaders that will arise during this season in the life our nation.

I hope for leadership that is not all-knowing. We would benefit from leadership that recognizes that as individuals we do not have the answer to every question as it relates to police and citizen interaction.

I hope for leadership that is not individualistic. We would benefit from leadership that recognizes that no one truly benefits when leadership is focused on personal agendas and/or personal desires to increase individual profiles.

I hope for leadership that is not opportunistic and "me" centered. We all benefit when leadership recognizes their position is not a photo opportunity but a service opportunity.

I hope for leadership that will seek the greater good of the entire community and not a singular people group.

I hope for leadership that will be collaborative and seek the input and opinion of people outside their own particular group in order to reach the overall goal of benefiting the entire community and moving everyone into a positive direction of justice and truth.

I hope for leadership that will seek to find peace instead of giving in to anger, hate or fear so that one group gets its way. To that end, I not only hope for these things, but continue my working toward the process of healing, learning from past mistakes, and developing a plan for future collaborative success. I offer the ideas found in this book in the name of justice, peace and reconciliation.

It is my desire that my life and work will continue to serve as an inspiration for future leaders who are faced with circumstances that will not only change them, but entire communities for the better.

Postscript:
What Police Officers Want From YOU...

A compassionate and informed citizenry is also an important contribution to the issue at hand, beginning with the challenges of being an officer. What can civilians do to be a help, and not a hindrance, to aid Police in performing their duty to protect and serve? To that end, I share the comments of two officers who weighed in on the topic, and have this to say:

OFFICER #1:

One of the biggest misconceptions people have is related to why someone would choose to become a Police Officer. None of us will become rich. You will miss out on important aspects in your personal life. There is a high probability that you will suffer serious injury and or possible death. The general line of thinking is that someone becomes a police officer because he was bullied, equate being a police offier as having "power," or he wasn't suited for other kinds of work. The fact is, a vast majority choose this profession because they see it as a way of giving back and making society a better place.

The things we deal with on a daily basis can potentially change our outlook and how we view others. Just like that one bad experience you had with an officer taints your view of all officers, imagine seeing basically the worst in people and man's inhumanity to his fellow man on a regular basis. The officer is also human and can, and will, eventually have his views change. It is almost inevitable that officers, based on

43

what they see day in and day out, will become cynical and begin to mostly see the worst in people.

The bad cop is the exception and not the rule. As much as society hates police corruption, good officers who took this job for the right reasons hate it even more. The rift that has been created between police and the communities they serve becomes bigger with each incident. This rift must be repaired and the trust must be won back, but there is no magic bullet solution to doing this. It takes time and understanding on both parts.

Officers need more cooperation from society. It begins and ends with you.

Neighborhoods are plagued by crime. As much as we want to make these neighborhoods safer, we (the officers) cannot do it alone. I cannot stress enough how much of a cooperative effort it takes to reduce crime. Officers and citizens alike have to invest in the community. Citizens cannot be complacent in this strategy. All too often when a crime occurs, no one wants to get involved. There are many instances where 20 people are outside when an incident occurs, however, not one of these individuals sees anything when questioned later by Officers!

Politics and Policing should be kept separate. In my years in law enforcement. I've that most decisions are made to be politically correct. However, the politically correct solution is usually not the best solution. Political decision making opens the doors for ineffective solutions. These solutions are more often than not a "band aid placed on a gaping wound" and end up costing more in the long run.

We all need to stop underestimating, and shortcutting, the job. To effectively reduce crime costs money and commitment. All too often managers of police departments have to do more with less, which is detrimental to all. Corners are cut when it comes to recruitment, training, and retention.

When these corners are cut you have a force that potentially is not capable of handling the rigors of this job skillfully and emotionally. Cutting corners is also the first step that allows those few "bad apples" to slip through the cracks. I believe that pay and benefits for officers should be increased drastically. However, as a caveat, I also believe that a four year degree should also be required, in the least, more training.

OFFICER #2

I wish citizens understood what a "Deadly Force" encounter was. This could help with police citizen relations. A gun is NOT an instrument of warning. We are not trained to shoot to wound. This is NOT television. Also, Tasers do not work under certain circumstances and they cannot be deployed as a first option in many situations.

"Militarization," while unappealing from an image standpoint, is sometimes necessary. Of course, the equipment must be deployed and used properly. But it IS necessary sometimes. Ours is not a warm and fuzzy profession. We are in place to deal with the least desirable and most dangerous aspects of society. That means that things can get rough and most dangerous.

It is ironic that we're asked to adhere to a strict set of rules and regulations while dealing with people whose primary goal is to IGNORE rules and regulations. Sometimes it would be better if activists and other citizens simply got out of the way, and let us do our jobs. Cops that go too far should be dealt with. But sometimes things can get rough out there: Stay out of the way, and let the Officers do their job.

I have a few suggestions for citizens that can help police officers do their jobs better. First, do not call 911 anonymously or refuse to let us call you back. It simply isn't necessary in the cell phone era. Officers cannot conduct a thorough investigation without having all the facts, and I cannot obtain those facts without asking questions. If you truly want to improve things in your neighborhood, let us talk to you. Cell phones mean that we don't have to walk up to your doorstep. Many citizens will call 911, but then say they do not want to get involved. Once you decide to call 911, you are involved.

Next, please explore all options for non-law enforcement situations before contacting the police. Dogs running loose, wires down, trees down, manhole covers missing—there is a city agency that handles these things. Calling the police to solve the problem simply takes manpower away from where it may be more urgently needed. Take a few minutes to locate the appropriate agency.

And, please understand that calling police does not guarantee that things will go your way. The role of an officer is to enforce the law, not to necessarily endorse your position or appease you.

About the Author

Terrell Carter served as a police officer for the City of St. Louis for five years. After leaving the department, he has served in various professional capacities, including as construction project manager, Executive Director of two community-based organizations, and as a college instructor.

He is a contributor to *Ethics Daily* and *Baptist News Global.*

Terrell has earned undergraduate, graduate, and post-graduate degrees in Biblical Studies and Organizational Leadership, Arts Management and Leadership, and Theology. He is a candidate for the degree of Doctor of Ministry in Congregational Health.

Terrell also serves as consultant and coach for community engagement and organizational effectiveness for nonprofit and for-profit organizations.

Mr. Carter is a sought after consultant and speaker in a number of areas, including issues on race and human relations, the dynamics of oppression, improving police-citizen interactions and community engagement, and, understanding and resolving the racial divide.

Terrell can be contacted at www.terrellcarter.net.

Follow him on twitter @tcarterstl.

Other Books by Bettie Youngs Book Publishers

The Story of Millard and Linda Fuller, Founders of Habitat for Humanity and The Fuller Center for Housing

Bettie B. Youngs

Everyone has heard of Habitat for Humanity, the faith-based housing initiative that has built homes for more than a million of the world's poor. Many are familiar with its founders, Millard and Linda Fuller. But few know the amazing love story behind the movement—a story that began accidentally and will conclude in a world forever changed by its impact.

By age 29, Millard Fuller was a self-made millionaire. But that success came at a cost. He never took a family vacation, had kids he barely knew, and a lonely wife who was about to leave him. Ultimately, realizing that he was about to lose what really mattered, Fuller reconciled with his wife and rearranged his priorities.

In 1965, the Fullers gave away their personal fortune and dedicated their lives to serving others, eventually founding Habitat for Humanity in 1976. In this capacity, the Fullers traveled the globe, receiving the praise of prime ministers and presidents, sharing meals with prisoners, and appealing for funds and volunteers. More important than any accolade or award were the homes they built and the hope they gave. The Fullers have done more for the cause of housing the poor than any other couple in history.

Eventually, a struggle for the reins of the most beloved nonprofit of our times would result in the firing of Millard and Linda by Habitat International's board of directors. This certainly didn't mean the end to their vision—the Fullers would rebound, continuing to support local Habitat affiliates and beginning The Fuller Center for Housing, determined to pursue their dream of building for people everywhere simple, decent places to live.

ISBN: 978-0-9882848-8-3 • ePub: 978-1-936332-53-3

A Primal Wisdom

V. Frank Asaro

This brilliant and entertaining book ties up a lot of loose ends and connects the dots on current thought about life, politics and economics. It lights up why we do what we do and explains how nature relates to the cooperative and competitive traits of humankind—to the order and chaos of the universe. It gives us a dynamic equation for synthesizing cooperative-order with competitive- chaos. It teaches the universal law of co-opetition. It shows us very simply how we can vastly improve our lives, our systems, our politics, our economies, and our relationships at home and between the peoples of the world. And, it shows us how we can do this, yet keep our good faith-rational principles and keep our freedom or build greater freedom.ct.

ISBN: 978-1-940784-23-6 • ePub: 978-1-940784-22-9

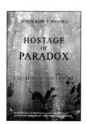

Hostage of Paradox: A Qualmish Disclosure

John Rixey Moore

Few people then or now know about the clandestine war that the CIA ran in Vietnam, using the Green Berets for secret operations throughout Southeast Asia. This was not the Vietnam War of the newsreels, the body counts, rice paddy footage, and men smoking cigarettes on the sandbag bunkers. This was a shadow directive of deep-penetration interdiction, reconnaissance, and assassination missions conducted by a selected few Special Forces units, deployed quietly from forward operations bases to prowl through agendas that, for security reasons, were seldom understood by the men themselves.

Hostage of Paradox is the first-hand account by one of these elite team leaders.

"Deserving of a place in the upper ranks of Vietnam War memoirs." —**Kirkus Review**

"Read this book, you'll be, as John Moore puts it, 'transfixed, like kittens in a box.'"
—**David Willson, Book Review, The VVA Veteran**

ISBN: 978-1-936332-37-3 • ePub: 978-1-936332-33-5

The Maybelline Story
And the Spirited Family Dynasty Behind It

Sharrie Williams

A fascinating and inspiring story, a tale both epic and intimate, alive with the clash, the hustle, the music, and dance of American enterprise.

"A richly told story of a forty-year, white-hot love triangle that fans the flames of a major worldwide conglomerate." —**Neil Shulman, Associate Producer,** *Doc Hollywood*

"Salacious! Engrossing! There are certain stories so dramatic, so sordid, that they seem positively destined for film; this is one of them." —*New York Post*

ISBN: 978-0-9843081-1-8 • ePub: 978-1-936332-17-5

On Toby's Terms

Charmaine Hammond

On Toby's Terms is an endearing story of a beguiling creature who teaches his owners that, despite their trying to teach him how to be the dog they want, he is the one to lay out the terms of being the dog he needs to be. This insight would change their lives forever.

"This is a captivating, heartwarming story and we are very excited about bringing it to film." —**Steve Hudis, Producer**

ISBN: 978-0-9843081-4-9 • ePub: 978-1-936332-15-1

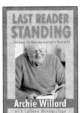

Last Reader Standing
... The Story of a Man Who Learned to Read at 54

Archie Willard
with Colleen Wiemerslage

The day Archie lost his thirty-one year job as a laborer at a meat packing company, he was forced to confront the secret he had held so closely for most of his
life: at the age of fifty-four, he couldn't read. For all his adult life, he'd been able to skirt around
the issue. But now, forced to find a new job to support his family, he could no longer hide from
the truth.

Last Reader Standing is the story of Archie's amazing journey of becoming literate at middle age,
struggling with the newfound knowledge of his dyslexia. From the little boy who was banished to
the back of the classroom because the teachers labeled him "stupid," Archie emerged to becoming
a national figure who continues to enlighten professionals into the world of the learning disabled.
He joined Barbara Bush on stage for her Literacy Foundation's fundraisers where she proudly
introduced him as "the man who took advantage of a second chance and improved his life."

This is a touching and poignant story that gives us an eye-opening view of the lack of literacy in
our society, and how important it is for all of us to have opportunity to become all that we can
be—to have hope and go after our dreams.

At the age of eighty-two, Archie continues to work with literacy issues in medicine and consumer-
ism.

"Archie . . . you need to continue spreading the word." **—Barbara Bush, founder of the
Literacy Foundation, and First Lady and wife of George H. W. Bush, the 41st President of the United States**

ISBN: 978-1-936332-48-9 • ePub: 978-1-936332-50-2

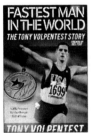

Fastest Man in the World
The Tony Volpentest Story

Tony Volpentest
Foreword by Ross Perot

Tony Volpentest, a four-time Paralympic gold medalist and five-time world
champion sprinter, is a 2012 nominee for the Olympic Hall of Fame. This
inspirational story details his being born without feet, to holding records as
the fastest sprinter in the world.

"This inspiring story is about the thrill of victory to be sure—winning gold—but it is also a
reminder about human potential: the willingness to push ourselves beyond the ledge of our
own imagination. A powerfully inspirational story." **—Charlie Huebner, United States
Olympic Committee**

ISBN: 978-1-940784-07-6 • ePub: 978-1-940784-08-3

Company of Stone

John Rixey Moore

With yet unhealed wounds from recent combat, John Moore undertook an unexpected walking tour in the rugged Scottish highlands. With the approach of a season of freezing rainstorms he took shelter in a remote monastery—a chance encounter that would change his future, his beliefs about blind chance, and the unexpected courses by which the best in human nature can smuggle its way into the life of a stranger. Afterwards, a chance conversation overheard in a village pub steered him to Canada, where he took a job as a rock drill operator in a large industrial gold mine. The dangers he encountered among the lost men in that dangerous other world, secretive men who sought permanent anonymity in the perils of work deep underground—a brutal kind of monasticism itself—challenged both his endurance and his sense of humanity.

With sensitivity and delightful good humor, Moore explores the surprising lessons learned in these strangely rich fraternities of forgotten men—a brotherhood housed in crumbling medieval masonry, and one shared in the unforgiving depths of the gold mine.

ISBN: 978-1-936332-44-1 • ePub: 978-1-936332-45-8

Blackbird Singing in the Dead of Night
What to Do When God Won't Answer

Updated Edition with Study Guide

Gregory L. Hunt

Pastor Greg Hunt had devoted nearly thirty years to congregational ministry, helping people experience God and find their way in life. Then came his own crisis of faith and calling. While turning to God for guidance, he finds nothing. Neither his education nor his religious involvements could prepare him for the disorienting impact of the experience. Alarmed, he tries an experiment. The result is startling—and changes his life entirely.

"Compelling. If you have ever longed to hear God whispering a love song into your life, read this book." —**Gary Chapman,** *NY Times* **bestselling author,** *The Love Languages of God*

ISBN: 978-0-9882848-9-0 • ePub: 978-1-936332-52-6

The Rebirth of Suzzan Blac

Suzzan Blac

A horrific upbringing and then abduction into the sex slave industry would all but kill Suzzan's spirit to live. But a happy marriage and two children brought love—and forty-two stunning paintings, art so raw that it initially frightened even the artist. "I hid the pieces for 15 years," says Suzzan, "but just as with the secrets in this book, I am slowing sneaking them out, one by one by one." Now a renowned artist, her work is exhibited world-wide. A story of inspiration, truth and victory.

"A solid memoir about a life reconstructed. Chilling, thrilling, and thought provoking."
—**Pearry Teo, Producer,** *The Gene Generation*

ISBN: 978-1-936332-22-9 • ePub: 978-1-936332-23-6

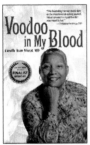

Voodoo in My Blood
A Healer's Journey from Surgeon to Shaman

Carolle Jean-Murat, M.D.

Born and raised in Haiti to a family of healers, US trained physician Carolle Jean-Murat came to be regarded as a world-class surgeon. But her success harbored a secret: in the operating room, she could quickly intuit the root cause of her patient's illness, often times knowing she could help the patient without surgery. Carolle knew that to fellow surgeons, her intuition was best left unmentioned. But when the devastating earthquake hit Haiti and Carolle returned to help, she had to acknowledge the shaman she had become.

"This fascinating memoir sheds light on the importance of asking yourself, 'Have I created for myself the life I've meant to live?'" —**Christiane Northrup, M.D., author of the New York Times bestsellers:** *Women's Bodies, Women's Wisdom*

ISBN: 978-1-936332-05-2 • ePub: 978-1-936332-04-5

Electric Living
The Science behind the Law of Attraction

Kolie Crutcher

An electrical engineer by training, Crutcher applies his in-depth knowledge of electrical engineering principles and practical engineering experience detailing the scientific explanation of why human beings become what they think. A practical, step-by-step guide to help you harness your thoughts and emotions so that the Law of Attraction will benefit you.

ISBN: 978-1-936332-58-8 • ePub: 978-1-936332-59-5

A World Torn Asunder
The Life and Triumph of Constantin C. Giurescu

Marina Giurescu, M.D.

Constantin C. Giurescu was Romania's leading historian and author. His granddaughter's fascinating story of this remarkable man and his family follows their struggles in war-torn Romania from 1900 to the fall of the Soviet Union. An "enlightened" society is dismantled with the 1946 Communist takeover of Romania, and Constantin is confined to the notorious Sighet penitentiary. Drawing on her grandfather's prison diary (which was put in a glass jar, buried in a yard, then smuggled out of the country by Dr. Paul E. Michelson—who does the FOREWORD for this book), private letters and her own research, Dr. Giurescu writes of the legacy from the turn of the century to the fall of Communism.

We see the rise of modern Romania, the misery of World War I, the blossoming of its culture between the wars, and then the sellout of Eastern Europe to Russia after World War II. In this sweeping account, we see not only its effects socially and culturally, but the triumph in its wake: a man and his people who reclaim better lives for themselves, and in the process, teach us a lesson in endurance, patience, and will—not only to survive, but to thrive.

"The inspirational story of a quiet man and his silent defiance in the face of tyranny."
—Dr. Connie Mariano, author of *The White House Doctor*

ISBN: 978-1-936332-76-2 • ePub: 978-1-936332-77-9

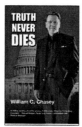

Truth Never Dies

William C. Chasey

A lobbyist for some 40 years, William C. Chasey represented some of the world's most prestigious business clients and twenty-three foreign governments before the US Congress. His integrity never questioned. All that changed when Chasey was hired to forge communications between Libya and the US Congress. A trip he took with a US Congressman for discussions with then Libyan leader Muammar Qadhafi forever changed Chasey's life. Upon his return, his bank accounts were frozen, clients and friends had been advised not to take his calls.

Things got worse: the CIA, FBI, IRS, and the Federal Judiciary attempted to coerce him into using his unique Libyan access to participate in a CIA-sponsored assassination plot of the two Libyans indicted for the bombing of Pan Am flight 103. Chasey's refusal to cooperate resulted in a six-year FBI investigation and sting operation, financial ruin, criminal charges, and incarceration in federal prison.

"A chilling narrative about the abuses of state power. Intriguing! Compelling. Important."
—Michael Reagan, Radio Host, Author, Commentator and Political Strategist

"An unprecedented first hand look into the chilling world of Libyan Leader Muammar Qadhafi by the man who risked it all to resolve the dispute between the United States and Libya over the Lockerbie bombing. This is sure to be an unforgettable motion picture."
—Peter Tomaszewicz, Producer, Truth Never Dies

ISBN: 978-1-936332-46-5 • ePub: 978-1-936332-47-2

54

The Girl Who Gave Her Wish Away

Sharon Babineau
Foreword by Craig Kielburger

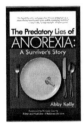

The Children's Wish Foundation approached lovely thirteen-year-old Maddison Babineau just after she received her cancer diagnosis. "You can have anything," they told her, "a Disney cruise? The chance to meet your favorite movie star? A five thousand dollar shopping spree?"

Maddie knew exactly what she wanted. She had recently been moved to tears after watching a television program about the plight of orphaned children. Maddie's wish? To ease the suffering of these children half-way across the world. Despite the ravishing cancer, she became an indefatigable fundraiser for "her children." In The Girl Who Gave Wish Away, her mother reveals Maddie's remarkable journey of providing hope and future to the village children who had filled her heart.

A special story, heartwarming and reassuring.

ISBN: 978-1-936332-96-0 • ePub: 978-1-936332-97-7

The Predatory Lies of Anorexia
A Survivor's Story

Abby D. Kelly

"I want...I want you to think I am the smartest, the thinnest, the most beautiful..."

With these words, Abby Kelly encapsulates the overwhelming struggle of her 15-year bout with anorexia. Abby lays bare the reality of anorexia, beginning in her teenage years, when the predatory lies of the disease took root in her psyche as she felt pressured from family and peers for not being "enough." In her quest for a greater sense of personal power, she concludes "I'll be 'more', but it will be on my terms."

Her reasoning is a classic example as to why and how eating disorders dig in and persist as long as they do.

From this new self-awareness, Abby targets her body as the agent to show others that she is disciplined and focused. She sets out to restrict her food intake and adheres to an extreme schedule of exercise. While others close to Abby see a person who is dangerously thin, Abby, in fact, derives a sense of personal achievement from her weight loss.

Abby exposes the battles, defeats, and ultimate triumph—taking the reader on a poignant odyssey from onset to recovery, including how she set out to fool the many who tried to help her, from dietitians to therapists, from one inpatient treatment center after another, and reveals not only the victim's suffering, but that of those who love her.

This raw and passionate story eloquently describes how Abby finally freed herself from this life-threatening condition, and how others can find courage and hope for recovery, too.

"This beautifully written book paints an exacting picture of Anorexia, one that is sure to help legions of those suffering from this most serious and life-threatening condition."
—**Amy Dardis, founder and editor of Haven Journal**

ISBN: 978-1-940784-17-5 • ePub: 978-1-940784-18-2

The Aspiring Actor's Handbook

Molly Cheek and Debbie Zip

Concise and straightforward, The Aspiring Actor's Handbook is written for curious and aspiring actors to help them make informed decisions while pursuing this exciting career.

Veteran actresses Molly Cheek and Debbie Zipp have culled the wit and wisdom of a wide array of successful actors, from Beth Grant to Dee Wallace, and collected the kind of mentoring perspective so many in the business wish they'd had when they were just starting out. Get insider information and real-life experiences and personal stories that range from how to get your foot in the door to becoming a career actor. Get the inside scoop from successful veteran actors on how to work with agents and unions; manage finances; prepare for auditions; cope with rejection—and success—and much more.

ISBN: 978-1-940784-12-0 • ePub: 978-1-940784-02-1

News Girls Don't Cry

Melissa McCarty

Today the host of ORA TV's Newsbreaker, and now calling Larry King her boss, Melissa McCarty worked her way up through the trenches of live television news. But she was also running away from her past, one of growing up in the roughest of neighborhoods, watching so many she knew—including her brother—succumb to drugs, gangs, and violence. It was a past that forced her to be tough and streetwise, traits that in her career as a popular television newscaster, would end up working against her.

Every tragic story she covered was a grim reminder of where she'd been. But the practiced and restrained emotion given to the camera became her protective armor even in her private life where she was unable to let her guard down—a demeanor that damaged both her personal and professional relationships. In News Girls Don't Cry, McCarty confronts the memory-demons of her past, exploring how they hardened her—and how she turned it all around.

An inspiring story of overcoming adversity, welcoming second chances, and becoming happy and authentic.

"A battle between personal success and private anguish, a captivating brave tale of a woman's drive to succed and her tireless struggle to keep her family intact. The reader is pulled into Melissa's story… an honest account of the common battle of addiction." —**Susan Hendricks, CNN Headline News Anchor**

ISBN: 978-1-936332-69-4 • ePub: 978-1-936332-70-0

MR. JOE
Tales from a Haunted Life

Joseph Barnett and Jane Congdon

Do you believe in ghosts? Joseph Barnett didn't, until the winter he was fired from his career job and became a school custodian. Assigned the graveyard shift, Joe was confronted with a series of bizarre and terrifying occurrences.

"Thrilling, thoughtful, elegantly told. So much more than a ghost story." —**Cyrus Webb, CEO, Conversation Book Club**

IISBN: 978-1-936332-78-6 • ePub: 978-1-936332-79-3

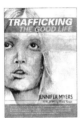

Trafficking the Good Life

Jennifer Myers

Jennifer Myers had worked hard toward a successful career as a dancer in Chicago. But just as her star was rising, she fell for the kingpin of a drug trafficking operation. Drawn to his life of excitement, she soon acquiesced to driving marijuana across the country, making easy money she stacked in shoeboxes and spent like an heiress. Only time in a federal prison made her face up to and understand her choices. It was there, at rock bottom, that she discovered that her real prison was the one she had unwittingly made inside herself and where she could start rebuilding a life of purpose and ethical pursuit.

"In her gripping memoir Jennifer Myers offers a startling account of how the pursuit of an elusive American Dream can lead us to the depths of the American criminal underbelly. Her book is as much about being human in a hyper-materialistic society as it is about drug culture. When the DEA finally knocks on Myers' door, she and the reader both see the moment for what it truly is—not so much an arrest as a rescue." —**Tony D'Souza, author of Whiteman and Mule**

ISBN: 978-1-936332-67-0 • ePub: 978-1-936332-68-7

Law of Attraction for Teens

How to Get More of the Good Stuff, and Get Rid of the Bad Stuff!

Christopher Combates

Whether it's getting better grades, creating better relationships, getting into college, or attracting a special someone, the Law of Attraction works! Aligning goals with your intentions enables you to create a better life. Written for teens, this engaging book will help teens to set purposeful goals, and to think, act, andcommunicate in the most positive way possible.

ISBN: 978-1-936332-29-8• ePub: 978-1-936332-30-4

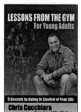

Lessons from the Gym For Young Adults

5 Secrets for Being in Control of Your Life

Chris Cucchiara

As a teen, Chris Cucchiara's life was a mess. Then he discovered the gym and he was transformed inside and out. Says Chris, "The gym taught me discipline, which led to achieving goals, which started a cycle of success." A much-admired high-performance coach for teens, in this book, Chris share his guiding principles on how to: develop mental toughness (a life without fear, stress, and anger); become and stay healthy and fit; build an "athlete for life" mentality that stresses excellence; and, set and achieve goals that matter.

ISBN: 978-1-936332-38-0 • ePub: 978-1-936332-34-2

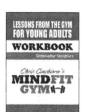

Lessons from the Gym For Young Adults

Workbook

Chris Cucchiara

A SUCCESS WORKBOOK FOR YOUNG ADULTS (ages 12-20) Do you lack self-confidence or have a difficult time making decisions? Do you sometimes wonder what is worth doing? Do you ever have a tough time feeling a sense of purpose and belonging? Chris shares his expertise of mastering success principles and shows you how to: Discover your real passion and purpose in life, which provides the drive, ambition and determination to overcome your limiting beliefs, fears, stress, and anger; Feel more in control of your life; Build your confidence and self-esteem; Build an athlete for life mentality that stresses leadership and excellence as a mindset; and, Stay motivated and set and achieve goals.

ISBN: 978-1-940784-16-8

Skin, Hair & Nail Care for Teens and Young Adults

Jennifer L. Youngs

There is nothing worse than waking up with a big zit on your face the day you have to give a report in front of the entire class! It's true, the first thing someone notices about you is your skin, hair and nails—indicators of how you take care of yourself. But good grooming is more than skin-deep: caring for

your skin, hair and nails helps you stay healthy and looking your very BEST at all times.

Consider this book your TOTAL Guide to everything you need to know about having healthy and beautiful skin, hair and nails!

ISBN: 978-1-940784-33-5• ePub: 978-1-940784-32-8

Confidence & Self-Esteem for Teens

Jennifer L. Youngs

Confidence & Self-Esteem for Teens is about the ways that beauty manifests from within. Have you ever run across someone who looked pretty, but undid her beauty by the way she acted or treated others?

Compare that to someone who is thoughtful, confident and comfortable with herself and as a result, has a lovely presence about her.

This book shows you how to let your inner beauty shine through—things like the secrets of serenity, steps for staying cool under pressure, building your self-esteem, drawing security from loving others, setting goals and feeling purposeful—and more.

ISBN: 978-1-940784-35-9 • ePub: 978-1-940784-34-2

Health & Fitness for Teens

Jennifer L. Youngs

Health & Fitness for Teens covers a most essential topic for teens: having a healthy body, liking your body and being fit. It's also a time of constant change. We can feel like we're just getting to know who we are when suddenly we are someone totally different. This book uncovers some of the myths teens have for comparing themselves to a standard other than their own, and covers some very important ground on how to best take care of themselves so as to look and feel their very best.

ISBN: 978-1-940784-33-5• ePub: 978-1-940784-32-8

Bettie Youngs Book Publishers

If you are unable to order books from your local bookseller, or online from Amazon or Barnes & Noble, or from Espresso, or, Read How You Want, or wholesaler Baker & Taylor, you may order directly from the publisher at Sales@BettieYoungsBooks.com.

VISIT OUR WEBSITE AT:
www.BettieYoungsBooks.com

CPSIA information can be obtained at www.ICGtesting.com
Printed in the USA
LVOW06s1005230815

451200LV00004B/588/P